EASY GUITAR TUNES

Anthony Marks

Designed by Doriana Berkovic
Edited by Jenny Tyler

Illustrated by Simone Abel
and Kim Blundell

Music selected, arranged and edited by Anthony Marks
New compositions by Anthony Marks
Guitar advisor: Mark Marrington
Music setting: Andrew Jones

About this book

You will already know some of these tunes, though others might be less familiar. Some of them were written specially for this book. If you have a computer, you can listen to all the tunes on the Usborne Quicklinks Website to hear how they go. Just go to **www.usborne-quicklinks.com** and enter the keywords "easy guitar tunes", then follow the simple instructions.

At the start of every piece there is a picture in a circle. Each picture has a sticker to match it in the middle of the book. Use the stickers to show when you have learned a piece.

Contents

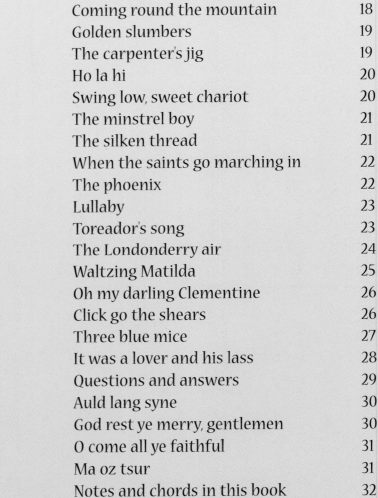

Guitar reminders

Here are some hints to help you enjoy guitar playing more. You can read these first, or go straight to the music on page 4 and come back here if you want some reminders.

If you need to know the fingering for a particular note, there is a chart on page 32 showing how to play all the notes in this book.

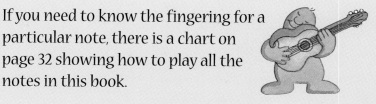

Getting comfortable

When you play the guitar, it is important to feel relaxed so that your fingers can move easily. Experiment until you find a position that feels right for you. To start with, it may be easiest to rest the guitar on your right leg, as shown below.

For some of the pieces, you will need to watch your left-hand fingers carefully. To make this easier, rest the guitar on your left leg (see below). Raise your left leg a little (you can use a special support for this). To look at your fingers, lean forward slightly.

Rest your right arm on top of the guitar.

Make sure the guitar is upright (not sloping forwards or backwards).

The guitar neck should be level or pointing slightly upwards.

Keep your back straight but not stiff.

Sit on the front part of the chair.

You could use a support for your left foot.

Left hand and fingers

Hold your left thumb straight out. Place it on the back of the guitar neck, about in line with the second fret.
  Curve your fingers over the strings so that when you press them down your fingertips are at right angles to the strings.

Press the strings firmly just to the left of the fretwire.

Your fingernails need to be fairly short.

Keep your hand and wrist relaxed.

Don't press too hard.

Plucking the strings

To play the tunes in this book, you need to pluck the strings in different ways. For most of the pieces, pluck with your index and middle fingers. Keep each finger straight. Pull upwards on the string, plucking towards your face, and let your finger rest on the next string. This is called rest stroke. In other pieces you will need a style of playing called free stroke. Keep your fingers curved

and pluck outwards, away from the guitar.
  For some of the pieces you need to use your thumb. Keep it straight, and pluck the string by pushing downwards, away from your face. Make sure only your thumb moves, not your whole hand.

Liza Jane

Try this old American tune a few different ways. Does it sound best fast or slow? Loud or quiet? Smooth or spiky?

The last rose of summer

This song was written by Thomas Moore, an Irish poet and composer who lived from 1779 to 1852. Watch out for the G sharp - use string 3, fret 1, finger 1.

4

Alouette

This is a French nursery rhyme, but it may first have been sung by French people in Canada in the 18th century. "Alouette" is the French word for "skylark".

Amazing grace

This tune became famous as a hymn in America, but it was first published around 1790 in England by a man named John Newton.

Andante

Men of Harlech

"Men of Harlech" is an old Welsh song. It is about a battle that took place in the 15th century, but the song was probably written many years later.

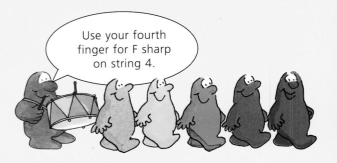

Use your fourth finger for F sharp on string 4.

Portsmouth

This sea shanty was popular in the 18th century. Portsmouth is a town on the south coast of England which is well known for its ships and dockyards.

Il pleut, bergère

"Il pleut, bergère" is French for "Shepherdess, it's raining". The song was written in the 1790s, when songs and plays about the countryside were very popular.

Tunes for two players

A tune for two players is called a duet. In a duet, one person plays the top line of music while someone else plays the lower one.

Before you try this, play your own part a few times until you know it well. (It can help to learn the other part too, so that you know what the other person is going to play.)

Then, when you play with someone else, count a few bars together before you start so that you begin at the same time. When you both know the music, try exchanging parts.

Pop! goes the weasel

This is an old English tune about the East End of London. Watch out for C sharp (string 2, fret 2, finger 2).

Cockles and mussels

This song was written in the 1880s by James Yorkston. It is about Dublin, the capital city of Ireland, and is sometimes known as "Molly Malone".

Left-hand fingers

In this book, there are numbers by some of the notes telling you which left-hand finger to use. Some of the fingerings may seem unfamiliar at first, but they will make the music easier to play. Try them slowly a few times until you get used to them.

Tingalayo

This tune comes from the Caribbean. Play the rhythms neatly and precisely. Make the accented notes a little louder than the ones around them.

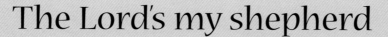

The Lord's my shepherd

This hymn tune was written by Jessie Irvine, who lived from 1836 to 1887. It is also known as "Crimond", the town in Scotland where Irvine lived.

Look out for D sharp - string 2, fret 4, finger 4.

Yellow bird

"Yellow bird" is a tune from Jamaica, an island in the Caribbean. Play the rhythms carefully and don't rush. See page 7 for more about tunes for two players.

Right-hand fingers

Play parts of "Yellow bird" with a mixture of right-hand thumb and fingers instead of just fingers. Play any notes on strings 4, 5 and 6 with your thumb. Play notes on strings 1, 2 and 3 with your index and middle fingers, using free stroke (see page 3).

Autumn

This tune is from "The Four Seasons", a set of pieces by an Italian composer, Antonio Vivaldi. Make the quiet notes a little shorter than the loud ones to get a good contrast.

Welcome friends

"Welcome friends" is a French-Canadian folk tune. Watch out for the G sharps, and make sure you don't rush the shortest notes.

The knight's song

This is a very old French tune. You have to play two strings at once. Find out more below.

If you use a plectrum, just play the top notes.

Slow and dignified

Playing two strings at once

To play two strings at once, you have to use your thumb and fingers at the same time. Play the lower notes with your thumb and the higher notes with your fingers, using free stroke (see page 3). Try playing both lines separately, then put them together. Play slowly at first until you get used to it.

Two white doves

You have to play the first line of this tune again at the end. Watch out for F sharp and G sharp.

Not too quickly

D.C. al Fine

Daisy, Daisy

Harry Dacre, an English songwriter, wrote this in 1892. It is about a couple being married and riding away on a tandem (a bicycle for two people).

Remember to count carefully when playing duets. Listen to the other player to make sure that you are playing together.

How far is it to Bethlehem?

Nobody knows who wrote this English Christmas Carol, but it is hundreds of years old. Play it slowly and gently.

The holly and the ivy

There are two versions of this carol. Both are old English tunes. Below you can see some of the words. Can you sing them to the tune opposite, too?

Oh, the holly and and the ivy
When they are both full grown
Of all the trees that are in the wood
The holly bears the crown.

Oh the rising of the sun
And the running of the deer
The playing of the merry organ
Sweet singing in the choir.

Patapan

This is a very old French Christmas song. You can add the lower notes with your thumb - see page 12 for more about this.

The holly and the ivy

For this 6/8 version, you have to feel two main beats in a bar, each divided into three. Which tune do you prefer?

Look out for the fingerings in this tune!

Billy boy

This tune is now more popular in America, but it was probably first sung in Britain. There are chord symbols in this tune - find out more below.

Chords

To accompany tunes, you can use chords (groups of notes played at the same time). Chords are shown by letters above the music.

Ask someone else to play the chords while you play the tune, then change over. (If there is just you, the tunes still work without the chords.)

For each chord, you need to learn where to put your left-hand fingers, and which strings to play. There are special diagrams to help you. The diagrams for the two chords to "Billy boy" (G and D) are shown below. There are more chords on page 32.

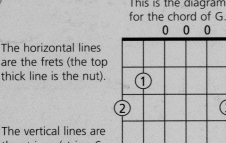

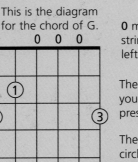

This is the diagram for the chord of G.

The horizontal lines are the frets (the top thick line is the nut).

The vertical lines are the strings (string 6 on the left).

0 means play the string without any left-hand fingers.

The circles show you where to press the strings.

The numbers in the circles show you which left-hand fingers to use.

This is the diagram for the chord of D.

X means don't play the string at all.

Chords need a little practice, but you will soon get used to them.

Playing chords with your right hand

When your left-hand fingers are in place, pluck the strings gently, moving across them with your thumb or first finger (or a plectrum). Start with the lowest string in the chord and move your hand downwards towards string 1.

This is called strumming. At first, strum each chord once every two beats, changing chord each time the symbol changes. Later you can try different strumming patterns.

Donkey riding

This is a popular Canadian tune though it
was probably first sung by French sailors
in the 18th century.

Song for you

This tune was written specially for this book.
You have to play two notes at once (see page 12).
Use your thumb for all the lower notes. See
page 32 for the chords to this tune.

My grandfather's clock

In this piece you need a new note - high A (string 1, fret 5, finger 4). To reach this, you need to move your whole hand up the neck of the guitar. This is called second position. Find out more on the opposite page.

Coming round the mountain

This is an old American folk tune. Play it all in second position. There are some chords to go with it, too (see page 16).

Golden slumbers

This is an old English lullaby. In this tune, you have to move from first to second position, and back again. Try this slowly at first until you get used to it.

The carpenter's jig

This old English dance uses both D natural and D sharp. In the fourth bar, you play D sharp with finger 3 because you are in second position.

Second position

To play in second position, move your whole hand one fret up the neck of the guitar. (Do this gently, without rushing.) In second position, finger 1 plays fret 2, finger 2 plays fret 3, and finger 3 plays fret 4.

In this book, whenever you have to move into second position, you will see the symbol "II" in the music. When you see the symbol "I", move down to first position again.

19

Ho la hi

This is a German folk tune. Play it quickly and lightly. There is a chord part too (see page 16). For this tune, try strumming a chord on every beat.

Swing low, sweet chariot

This song was first written down around 1905 by Harry Thacker Burleigh, a composer whose grandfather was a slave in the southern USA.

Follow the fingering very carefully.

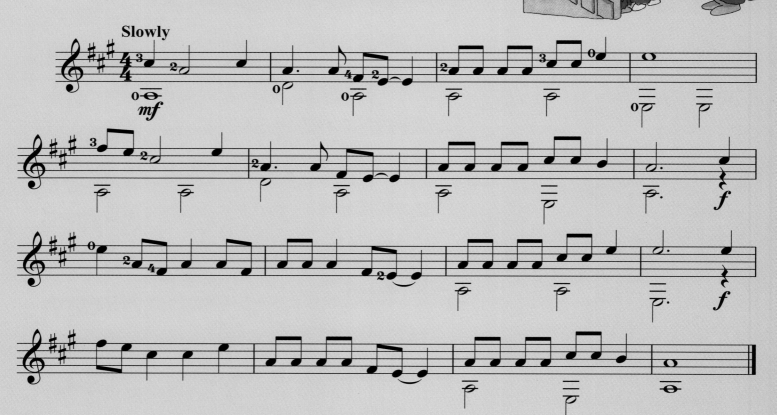

The minstrel boy

Nobody knows who wrote this Irish tune. It was first published in the 19th century, with words by Thomas Moore.

Like a march

The silken thread

The time signature changes from 3/4 to 2/4 in this German folk tune, so count carefully. It may help to clap the rhythm a few times before you start to play

Allegretto

When the saints go marching in

You can play this as a duet (see page 7) or the
top line on your own. This tune was first sung
by African slaves in the USA.

The phoenix

For this old English dance tune, make the
fast notes smooth and even. (Start slowly
and build up speed.)

Lullaby

This tune is by a German composer, Johannes Brahms. He lived from 1833 to 1897.

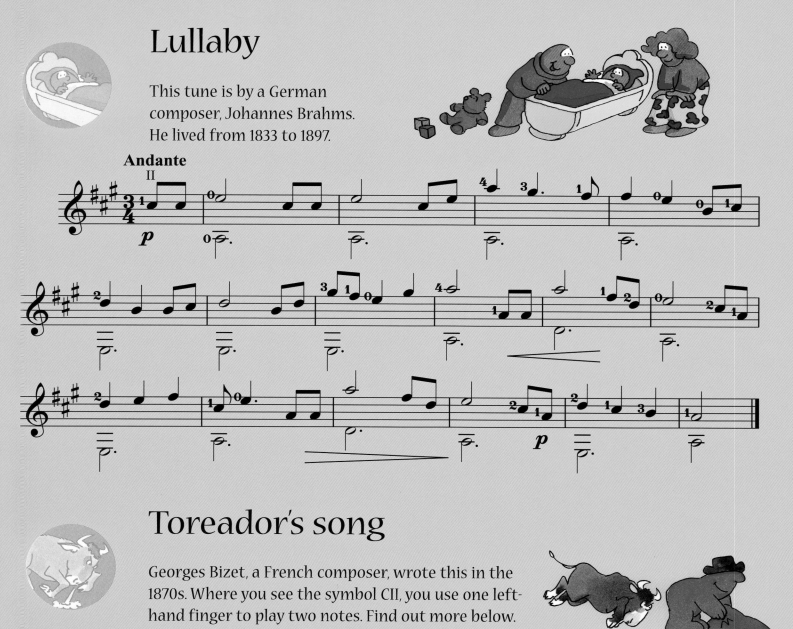

Toreador's song

Georges Bizet, a French composer, wrote this in the 1870s. Where you see the symbol CII, you use one left-hand finger to play two notes. Find out more below.

To play C sharp and F sharp in bar 7, flatten finger 1 of your left hand across strings 1 and 2 (at fret 2). This is called making a barre, or barring.

When the line above the music stops, let go of the barre.

23

The Londonderry air

This is an old Irish tune. Follow the fingering carefully around the high A in the second bar of the last line. Slide your fourth finger down from A to G.

finger 3 plays
C on string 3

Transposing

Below are three tunes from earlier in the book. Now their first lines are written out starting on different notes. Can you play the rest of each tune? (Look at the fingering chart on page 32 if you get stuck.)

Try starting some other tunes on different notes. This helps you to find your way around the guitar and to understand more about music. Changing notes like this is called transposing.

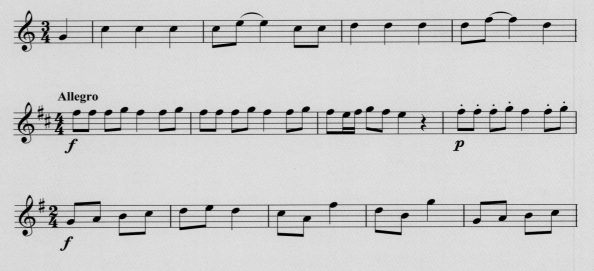

Cockles and mussels (page 8): start on G, string 3

Autumn (page 11): start on F sharp, string 1 and use second position

Ho la hi (page 20): start on G

Waltzing Matilda

"Waltzing Matilda" is an Australian song. It was written in 1895 by Banjo Patterson, though it is based on an older Scottish tune called "Craigielee".

Oh my darling Clementine

An American composer, Percy Montross, wrote this tune around 1880. Play the dotted notes very crisply.

Click go the shears

"Click go the shears" is an Australian song about sheep-shearing (cutting the wool off sheep).

There is a chord part for this tune. See page 32 for chord diagrams.

Three blue mice

This duet was written specially for this book. It is based on a well-known tune. Can you work out which one?

Blues

"Three blue mice" is in a style called blues. Blues began in the USA at the end of the 19th century. It is based on chains of chords called progressions. There are many blues chord progressions. The one on the right works with "Three blue mice". When you can play the duet, get someone else to try the chords.

At first, play each chord in the chart once and make it last for two beats. Then try strumming each chord twice (once per beat), moving down and back up across the strings. Can you think of other strumming patterns and rhythms too?

D	D	D	D
D	D	D	D7
G	G	G	G7
D	D	D	D
A	A	G	G7
D	A	D	D

Can you make up a new tune to go with these chords?

It was a lover and his lass

This was written by the English composer Thomas Morley. It was published in 1600, and was also used in Shakespeare's play "As you like it".

Questions and answers

This tune was written specially for this book. Once you know it, you can play it in lots of different ways - find out more below.

Different ways to play "Questions and answers"

Can you hear how the first bar sounds like a question, while the second is like an answer? You could make up your own answers instead of the ones in the music. At first, use the same notes but change the rhythm, or use the same rhythm and change the notes.

All the odd-numbered bars are questions. Try to make up answers to all of them. Then play the tune with a mixture of your own answers and the ones already there. Ask someone else to play the question bars while you invent the answers, then change over.

The music on the right can be played as an accompaniment, all the way through the tune. Ask a friend to play it.

Now start on open D (string 4). The first two bars been have done for you here. Can you make up answers when you start on this note?

Can you do this starting on other notes, too?

29

Auld lang syne

This is a Scottish tune. It was first written down in the 18th century by the poet Robert Burns. People sing it on New Year's Eve. The title means "Old times".

God rest ye merry, gentlemen

This Christmas song is very old, but it first became popular in the 19th century. Don't rush the short notes.

O come all ye faithful

This tune was first sung in the 18th century, but nobody knows who wrote it. Play it all in second position.

Ma oz tsur

Jewish people sing this during Hannukah, a winter festival. "Ma oz tsur" means "Rock that shelters me".

Notes in this book

Below you can check how to play the notes used in this book. The staves show the notes and their names. The small numbers tell you which left-hand finger you normally use to play the note, putting finger 1 on fret 1, finger 2 on fret 2 and so on. The symbol 0 means that the note is an open string - you don't use any left-hand fingers. Underneath the staves, the string numbers tell you which string to use - string 6 is low E, string 1 is high E.

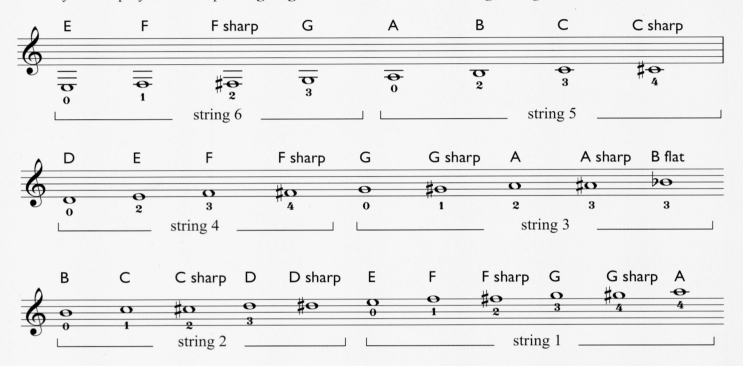

Chords

This chart shows you how to play the chords used in this book. The vertical lines are the strings (with the sixth string furthest to the left). The horizontal lines show the frets. The circles show you where to press your fingers, and the numbers in the circles show you which finger to use. An 0 above a string tells you to play an open string. A cross tells you not to play that string at all.

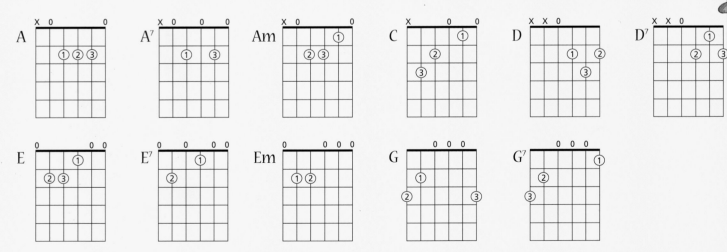

First published in 2004 by Usborne Publishing Ltd, Usborne House, 83-85 Saffron Hill, London ECIN 8RT, England.
www.usborne.com